Start a Successful Amazon FBA Business

Top 22 Mistakes to Avoid When Selling on Amazon FBA

By Paul D. Kings

No part of this book can be transmitted or reproduced in any form including print, electronic, photocopying, scanning, mechanical or recording without prior written permission from the author.

All information, ideas, and guidelines presented here are for educational purposes only. All readers are encouraged to seek professional advice when needed.

While the author has taken utmost efforts to ensure the accuracy of the written content, all readers are advised to follow information mentioned herein at their own risk. The author cannot be held responsible for any personal or commercial damage caused by misinterpretation of information or improper use of the information.

This page was left blank intentionally

This page was left blank intentionally

Table of Contents

This page was left blank intentionally

Preface

Mistakes happen. We are humans. First, we are babies and then little children. Some kids want to run before they can walk. They fall. They cry. They get up and try again. Little kids make little mistakes. Big kids, well, make big mistakes.

We are not machines. We make mistakes. But as we mature, we are always learning from our mistakes. And the greatest accomplishment of all is to learn from other people's mistakes.

We know deep inside that there is no escaping making mistakes in life. In business, we see that even when someone perfects a business, if they do not evolve with market expectations, the business will die. Think of Blockbuster Videos not adapting to what Netflix was doing. Businesses always have to change and adapt, to be profitable. Otherwise, they will lose out to the competition.

The Fulfilled by Amazon (FBA) program is not for everyone. Amazon FBA is where you can send inventory to Amazon, they store it in their warehouse, and when a customer orders your products, Amazon will pack and ship those items to your customers. Amazon gets their cut in the form of FBA fees, and you get the rest. The customer gets their product quickly; if they are Prime Subscribers, they will get their product in about two days, with free shipping. In theory, everybody wins.

Well actually, not everyone wins, or at least not everybody wins all the time. But I can assure you, Amazon **always** wins.

I have been selling on Amazon and eBay since 2007. I have been using Amazon FBA for a while and can let you in on some of my mistakes. The reason to read this book is not to wallow in pity and feel sorry for you or the next guy for making mistakes. The reason to read this book is to learn from those mistakes, and like the little child, get up and keep trying again.

We can learn from other people's mistakes, and decide not to make the same mistakes they did, so that we do not suffer the same consequences. Then again, we might still make some mistakes of our own, at that time what we need to do is to capture what is happening in our business. That way we can evaluate it and see what is working and what is not so that we can evolve our business strategy.

For more information about Amazon FBA, I invite you to read my first Amazon FBA book:

Making Money With Amazon FBA: Tips for Getting Started Selling, and Mistakes to Avoid (Making Money Online). This book is offered free at the end of this book for my readers.

Paul D. Kings

What is Amazon FBA

Amazon FBA or to give it, it's full name Fulfillment By Amazon, is a program set up by Amazon that allows you to use Amazon to warehouse and then send out your items (and also always you to sell your items on the Amazon Site). Amazon FBA is very simple, but at the same time is very powerful and can take your business to the next level for very low costs.

Imagine the scene, you are busy doing your product sourcing and have picked up some books, CD's DVD's, Home and Beauty items, a few new toys (yes items sold via Amazon FBA have to be either new or collectible). Now normally at the back of your mind you are thinking I wish I could buy more stock, but there is no more room at home. This is where Amazon FBA comes into play.

You come home and scan or list the items as usual into your Amazon selling account and a few clicks later, you print out some bar codes which you must put over the original product bar code on the item (Yes items will need to have a bar code or listed on the Amazon site). After a few more clicks and you print out a packing slip which goes in the box or boxes. You then book a pick-up from a carrier, and this does depend on where you live and how you pay for it.

As a side note, you can use Amazon's video tutorials on how to pack, label and ship items sent for the FBA program here.

Next you complete the order and wait for the order to be picked up and within days your items will be in the Amazon warehouse being sold for you, and you can sit back and bank the money. Amazon FBA deals with payments, shipping, and customer emails, you just need to source more stock and bank the money.

Yes there are some extra costs that Amazon charges but these are low, and the savings you make on the postage is fantastic - remember you are using Amazon's buying power. Also, no more queues in Post Offices.

Amazon Multi-Channel Fulfillment Services

Something else people do not realize is that you can use Amazon FBA to ship out to your eBay and other buyers. Yes Amazon stores the items and sends the items out for you!. And for a fraction of the cost, and in most cases, a lot cheaper than you can do.

You can also sell products on Amazon and not use their FBA service, so you ship your own products, but there are many advantages of using the FBA system, which will free up your time and provide a more automated business solution.

Amazon FBA may look similar to services that other drop shippers provide, but Amazon holds your own goods in one of their fulfillment centers. The service will send your goods anytime and to anywhere on your behalf. This system can be further integrated with your website to create a virtually fully automated system for sending Amazon your goods, and for Amazon shipping them to your customers.

You can learn about Amazon's Multi-Channel Fulfillment services here, again with easy to follow videos and useful information.

So why should you consider using Amazon's system?

Here are some of the key points to the FBA system:

- You can sell almost anything on Amazon, or through your website and have them pack and send.

- By automating your website sales with Amazon it means the business can run on autopilot, and you can take time away if you choose, and your business still functions.

- Send all your stock to Amazon and they will handle everything, all you have to do is collect your profits.

- Amazon is now outranking eBay on Alexa for traffic, they are a major competitor to eBay.

- Some eBay sellers are using the Amazon FBA to ship goods sold through eBay.

You can sell almost anything as I stated before. For example as well as books, Amazon has categories similar to eBay which cover just about anything you can think of for the home, garden, office, clothing, sports and so on. We will later discuss some categories, products, and brands that you might not be able to sell when using Amazon.

To learn more about Amazon FBA: read my book:

Making Money With Amazon FBA:
Tips for Getting Started Selling, and Mistakes to
Avoid
by Paul D. Kings

Top 22 Mistakes to Avoid When Selling on Amazon FBA

Mistake #1: Not keeping track of your business expenses

When starting out working Amazon FBA or any business, you should keep track of your expenses. First of all, keeping track of your expenses will let you know if you are making a profit or not. Second, of all, you can claim your expenses on your taxes.

Additionally, you should save receipts and invoices of all your expenses. This is important because should you get audited by the IRS you will have proof of what your expenses were.

Mistake #2: Selling Junk on Amazon FBA

You should not sell any used items on Amazon FBA, even if you can. If you sell used electronics and the item does not work properly and returns it, your defect rate can go up. If your defect rate goes up, it will have a negative effect on your account.

Also, with defective merchandise, you will get negative reviews, which again will affect your standing with Amazon. In the short term, a bad defect rate or negative feedback can determine whether buyers decide to buy from you and whether Amazon grants you the Buy Box. In the long run, having too many defect claims can push Amazon to close your seller account. Something you do not want.

Remember Amazon FBA is not like selling on eBay. Decide that you will only sell items on Amazon FBA that are new and come from reputable sources. This decision will help you in the long run. Even buying "new" items on eBay and sending it to Amazon can have its negative effects.

I once purchased a "new" Wifi Router from eBay that was at a third of the price of what it was selling with Prime (Amazon FBA). When I received it, in came in a new box and was in Shrink Wrap. I did not think much of it. I was hoping the item was really new and had no issues. I sent it to the Amazon warehouse, and the item sold. I made a good profit on it; or so I thought. A few days later, the customer who bought it, returned it as defective. I lost money on this sale.

Mistake #3: Only Looking at Sales Rank When Deciding What to Sell on Amazon

Amazon assigns a Best Seller Rank to most of its products. This number is updated hourly. In a particular category (let's say Toys & Games), all the products in that category are compared against each other and ranked, so that the best-sold item is ranked #1, and second best is ranked #2, and so on. This number changes hourly.

For most products sold on Amazon, the number of units sold in a month (or daily) could be calculated using the Jungle Scout Sales Estimator tool. You should use this tool before deciding if you should sell an item on Amazon.

On the other hand, sales rank is not everything. An item could have an apparently bad sales rank at the moment, however, have hundreds of good reviews. This means that even if the item is not selling well at the very moment, that could change later on. Having a lot of good reviews is social proof that the item has sold in the past. Maybe the item is seasonal, and sales will eventually pick up in Spring or the Winter, etc.

Mistake #4: Not looking at the Product Reviews

If you sell an item that has bad product reviews, this can mean two things for you. First, the product may not sell very one. Second, even if the product sells you will get a lot of returns. And as discussed before, you can end up with negative product reviews, negative seller feedback, a rapidly increasing defect rate, and finally problems with Amazon.

Make sure to look at the product reviews before buying an item and deciding to sell it on Amazon.

Mistake #5: Buying Deep instead of Wide
When you find a good deal on a product that is selling at a much higher price range on Amazon, you have to think; you could decide to go deep on a product. Going "deep" means that instead of buying just one or two units of a product, you will buy that product in high quantities and sell high on Amazon. The reasoning is clear: if you can make $10 profit on one item, you could make $100 profit on 10, and so on.

This mentality can work in your favor. But can also work against you. Imagine this scenario: you get to find out that Walmart has an item on sale, which is advertised on Walmart.com. You buy the product because the product has a good sales rank on Amazon, and is currently selling at a much higher price there. What can go wrong?

Well, for starters, if Amazon is selling the product itself, it will eventually figure out that a competitor is selling the product at a much lower price and will price match it. Amazon has eyes everywhere. Amazon can do this really fast. By the time you send your product to Amazon, you would have spent time and money shipping your products to Amazon.

It can take a week or more for Amazon to get your products into their warehouses and listed on its website. By the time your item is finally listed online, you could lose money. If you are competing against Amazon, you might have to sell the item at a lower price to make a sale. If you wait until Amazon goes out of stock, you might lose money on storage fees.

Secondly, if you find the discounted price online, it is likely other third party sellers can find out about this discount too. An item can look profitable now, and you might think that you could sell the item at the same price that you see online at that time.

However, other third party sellers are doing the same thing you are doing. You ship your items to Amazon, only to find out a week or two later that many other vendors are competing against you to get the Buy Box. They will sell their items cheap. It is possible they bought their items even cheaper than you and are making a profit.

Given these situations, the only way you could sell your products now is to lower the price, and thus lose money. You could decide to wait it out and sell when your competition has sold out. However, your competition might have tens, hundreds or even thousands of items in inventory. Therefore they will not go out of stock anytime soon. The result, you lower price to attract sales and end up losing money.

So what is the alternative? Well instead of buying "deep," you decide to buy "wide." That is, instead of purchasing a lot of the same SKU, you buy several different products. For example, instead of buying 10 Barbie dolls, you spread out your risk (and rewards) with 10 different types of toys. That way, if you lose money on one, hopefully, you won't lose money on the others, and maybe make a profit.

I have to be honest, selling with Amazon FBA is not for everyone. But for any business, there are risks and rewards. To be successful in any business, you will have to be patient, try different strategies and see what works and what does not work.

Keep reading this book. Discover what mistakes I or others have made and decide what you will do, hopefully avoiding those mistakes or finding a way to reduce the potential downfall of your decisions.

Mistake #6: Participating in a Race to The Bottom

When a seller decides to lower their price to make a sale, the other sellers can price match them or have their prices go even lower. Nobody wins. Everybody loses. Because the more a seller lowers its price, and then another does the same, back and forth, the price will end up very low. This is what's called a "Race to the bottom."

Before participating in this competition, you want to consider if the item is popular. If it is popular, you may be served better to wait until your competitors sell out, and then you can sell your item at a higher price than they did.

At any rate, you may want to calm down and make your pricing decisions slowly. In the end, you may have to lower your prices, and that may be the only way to sell your product. However, don't treat this is a game because this is not a game. In a game, losing means you get a do-over. In real life, you will end up losing money.

Take it slow, and figure out if you are going to price match a competitor or if you should wait things out.

Mistake #7: Holding on to items that are not selling well or selling at all

You see that retailers do what's called a clearance. For example, Walmart, Target and other stores, when certain holidays are over they will have merchandise on sale. What they are doing is making space on their shelves and aisles for newer merchandise. Merchandise that will sell well in that particular season.

As an Amazon FBA seller, you will encounter similar situations. You may have lots of inventory that is not selling well. You have to consider that every month you pay storage fees for having your merchandise at Amazon's warehouses. You will also pay long term storage fees every six months.

You need to take a look at your inventory and figure out what is selling and what is not. Figure out the losers. The losers here are items that are not selling and or have not sold for a very long time. Decide to lower the price of these items, until they sell. Or decide to have Amazon send them back to you or destroy them.

When removing items from the warehouse, you incur a small fee for either shipping them back to you or having them destroyed. If you have them shipped back to you, you could send them back to Amazon at a later date when the items may be selling better. Or you could sell the items at a garage sale, Craigslist, eBay or give them away to charity (and claim that on your taxes).

Mistake #8: Selling a Product Without Doing Proper Research

We already talked about the difference between going deep and going wide on a product. Sometimes you see a great special for a product at a store, or you get good prices from a manufacturer or distributor, and it seems that you can sell that product at a good profit.

What you should do next do is use Amazon Best Seller Rank along with tools like Jungle Scout Sales Estimator. You can also use tools like CamelCamelCamel.com or Keepa to look at the sales history and sales velocity of a product.

Before jumping in and buying a massive amount of a product, do the proper research. Make sure that you can sell the product a higher price. Study the competition. See if you can compete in that market. Study if Amazon has had the product in stock.

Whatever you do, make sure that you make your decisions based on research and not just at the spur of the moment. But also, learn from your mistakes. Take a look back at how you are doing and see if you can improve your buying/selling decisions next time. Any business requires that you become agile and adapt to changes in supply and demand.

Mistake #9: Not Paying Attention or Removing Negative Feedback

Sometimes people are not happy with the product they received. However, this is not your fault. If the product is not good, the customer should leave a product review. Not a negative seller feedback. If you find that people left you bad seller feedback due to a bad product, you can contact Amazon and have them remove the negative feedback.

Also, if a buyer left you bad feedback either by mistake (maybe they said some good things but left a one-star rating by mistake) or on purpose, see if you can ask the buyer directly to change the feedback or remove it. Through the Amazon system, you can contact the customer and see if you can come to an arrangement with them; you can offer them a full refund or replacement in lieu of the bad review. They might remove the feedback.

On the other hand, if a customer leaves bad seller feedback and is obviously threatening you to get a refund, contact Amazon seller support, as they should not use feedback as blackmail to get free merchandise. Amazon will likely remove the negative feedback.

You need to take care of your seller feedback. People that buy on Amazon are not inclined to leave seller feedback. You should try and increase your seller feedback by using tools like Feedback Genius. Feedback Genius will send out messages to your customers, at certain triggers, such as when they order, when they get their order and a few days or months after they get their order.

You can set up Feedback Genius with your store logo and custom HTML email template. You can setup your messages to automatically ask customers for product reviews and/or seller feedback. Feedback Genius has a 30-day trial. They also have a free plan where you can keep sending a limited number of emails to your customers even after the trial is over. If you do decide to pay for the service, it is very affordable.

Whatever tool you use, you need to keep on top of your seller feedback. When people try to buy from you, they look at the seller feedback, and if it's not good, they might pick your competition, even if your price is lower than theirs.

Try also to sell new merchandise or items that do not have a high percentage of returns (such as electronics). People might not be inclined to leave good feedback, but they are sometimes quick to leave bad reviews when they are not happy with a product or service.

Mistake #10: Not Getting Ungated In Certain Categories as Soon As Possible

You may know, Amazon has restrictions on certain categories. You want to make sure you can sell in as many categories as possible.

The following information comes from Amazon's website

What can I sell?

Open Categories

More than 20 categories are open for selling on Amazon; products in these categories can be listed without specific permission from Amazon. Some categories only allow listings for new products. Some categories have additional guidelines that sellers must follow.

Categories Requiring Approval

Products in categories requiring approval can be listed only with specific permissions from Amazon. Only sellers with a Professional Selling Plan subscription can sell in these categories. Amazon limits access to sell in these categories to help ensure that sellers meet standards for product and listing quality as well as other category-specific requirements. These standards help Amazon customers have confidence when buying in any category.

How to Request Approval

1. If you meet the requirements described in the table below, use the Contact us form to request approval.

2. Fill out the form to submit your request. You will receive an e-mail response in approximately three business days letting you know whether you've been approved to sell or requesting additional information.

Make sure to submit your requests and attempt to get approval to sell on as many categories as you can, even if you don't think you will ever sell in those categories. There may come a time in the future that you will want to sell in those categories for some reason, such as because you can get a good deal on a product in that category. If you are already approved to sell in that category, you will be able to list the item right away.

If you are approved to sell in certain categories, which are harder to get into, like Health & Beauty, you will have an advantage over your competitors who won't be able to sell in those categories.

Sometimes all it takes to get approval is to fill out a simple questionnaire, and boom you are automatically approved to sell in that category in a couple of minutes. Other times, you fill out a simple questionnaire, but you have to wait for an Amazon rep to approve your request. Other times, you will have to show receipts or invoices for items in that category; this is true for categories such as Groceries.

You will be served well by reading what other people have done to get approved. Do a google search to find advice or recommendations of companies that could help you get ungated in a particular category you want to sell on.

Mistake #11: Not Collecting Sales Tax

Legally you are required to collect sales tax at least in the state that you live in for customers that also live in that state. There's a lot of controversy as to whether you should also collect taxes for customers that live in the state where Amazon stores your inventory.

Some people say that you should collect taxes there. Others say that you don't have to. Either way, consult a CPA for advice on what to do there.

You can consult the TaxJar's website for more information about collecting taxes. TaxJar is a paid tool or service that you can use to help you collect taxes and send the the taxes that you collect to the state agencies.

When you have a lot of inventory for which you have to pay taxes, use a tool or service that can help you do that; using a tool not only will help you be in the clear with those states, but also save you time and money since each state has specific rules that you need to follow to collect and pay sales taxes.

Mistake #12: Not Keeping up with Amazon's Rules Changes

Amazon, like many big online businesses such as eBay, Google, YouTube, and others, is constantly changing their rules or terms. You want to make sure to keep up with whatever new rules or fees that Amazon has. Know what changes are coming down the pike. Be prepared. That way you can quickly adapt to the changes and still be profitable.

You have the option of getting mad at Amazon when they modify the rules for Amazon FBA sellers, or you can decide to adapt. Keep in mind that you are playing in Amazon's sandbox.

In the long term, you will do well by adapting to changes to whatever selling platform you are using, and that includes Amazon. If you do not adapt to changes, your business will certainly languish and die. If you adapt to changes, your business can grow and prosper.

Mistake #13: Spending Too Much Time manually Repricing.

This mistake applies to those that have a lot of inventory. To make money selling on Amazon you will have to keep on top of pricing so you can get the Buy Box. When people want to buy a product on Amazon, they will hit the "Add to Cart" or the "Buy now with 1-Click" buttons. They might not care who the buyer is they are getting their product from, as long as they get their 2-day free shipping with Prime.

You as the seller will have a chance of getting the Buy Box. Getting the Buy Box is influenced by many factors, one of them is participating in the Amazon FBA program, and another is having the lowest price or being within a certain percent of the lowest price of other FBA sellers. The more times you win the Buy Box, the more chances you have of making a sale.

Imagine that you have a few items, keeping up with pricing can easily be done manually. However, if you have thousands of products, in various categories, and if you reprice your products manually, you will be wasting a lot of time.

Some recommend that when you get over a couple of hundred SKUs (Stock Keeping Units in your inventory), you should use a repricing tool. Amazon itself has a free automatic repricing tool that you can use. This tool is in Beta. There are other repricers online that you can find out about, such as RepricerExpress. They may have a trial period that you can use to determine if you want to keep using that tool.

My advice is that you do not start using an automatic repricing tool. However, as you grow your inventory, you should research the pros and cons of using a repricer and what are the best-recommended tools. See what others say about these tools in the Seller Central Forums and other sites.

Mistake #14: Not sending enough items to sell on Amazon FBA

Not sending enough items to sell on Amazon FBA is the opposite of buying too much inventory.

It is a fact of life that the more items you list on any platform, whether it's eBay, Amazon, Craigslist, the more chances you have of making sales and the more money you can make.

From my personal experience, I suggest that when you start, start out small to see what works and what not, and don't invest any money you depend on and cannot lose risking. However, as you start growing and getting confidence using Amazon FBA, make sure to keep sending inventory to Amazon.

You want to "Feed the beast" as FBA sellers call Amazon. You do not want to stop sending inventory, unless you need to take time off due to a vacation or personal situation. But even then, you may want to plan on ways you can maybe hire somebody to help keep sending inventory to Amazon. It seems that the more you send to Amazon FBA, the more money you stand to make.

Mistake #15: Not diversifying your sourcing methods

There are many ways to source product to send inventory to Amazon: you can use:

- Retail stores
- Thrift stores
- Pawn shops
- Online stores
- Garage sales
- Craigslist
- OfferUp App
- Private Labeling
- Wholesale

You want to start diversifying your sourcing methods. Learn about new sourcing methods. Get good at a few but learn about them all. As time moves on, your competitors learn new things too. You have to stay ahead of the curve, and one way to do this is by diversifying your sourcing methods.

Even if you don't think you want to start doing something such as private labeling now, at least learn about it now since maybe that's the next thing that you will have to do to stay ahead of the competition. You may want to look into doing Wholesale, liquidation estate sales, etc. The point is that you diversify the ways you source and make money.

This tip can also apply to many other things you do with Amazon FBA. You want to stay ahead of your competition; always learning new things and adapting; reading and watching new trends in general.

Mistake #16: Not Networking or Learning from Others

One of the biggest mistakes that people make when they are doing something new is not networking with other people that are doing or have done what you want to do.

You can save a lot of time, and money, by networking with like-minded people, watching YouTube videos, joining Facebook groups, the Amazon Seller Central forums, Amazon FBA related subreddits, etc.

There are many nice and helpful people out there, online, that can help you as you begin your journey with Amazon FBA. You don't have to do this by yourself. You can learn from others, and in time you will pay it forward, and help others yourself.

Mistake #17: Not Upgrading to a Third Party Inventory Management Tool
As you start scaling your Amazon FBA business, you might keep track of your inventory using an Excel spreadsheet. Using Excel is good and enough at the beginning. However, as you grow using simple tools may not sustainable.

You need a third party tool like Inventory Labs. This tool can help you keep track of inventory and show how much profit you are making when you make a sale. Something that the free Amazon tools will not help you with. Yes, you could do all of this yourself with your spreadsheet, but it will take a lot of time to do it yourself. And we know, time is money.

When your business is growing is time to update your inventory management tool. An inventory tool such as Inventory Labs can help you when you do your taxes because it will assist you with your bookkeeping. There are other inventory tools out there, but I recommend Inventory Labs. It has a full 30-day trial.

Mistake #18: Not covering original product barcodes when sending products to Amazon

When sending products to Amazon, you should use a seller's label that Amazon provides to cover the products' original UPC code. Not doing so, can confuse the Amazon warehouse workers. They may not scan your seller's code and think the product should be setup as "stickerless commingled" inventory, meaning that they will put your product into a pile with other sellers' merchandise.

We have talked about this mistake of commingling inventory before. You should not do this because this means Amazon can ship other people's product to your customers and if those products are counterfeit, you are the one that will get in trouble with Amazon and may suspend your account without warning.

Make sure that before you send a product to Amazon, you cover all its UPC codes with your seller sticker or a blank sticker that simply covers the UPC to avoid potentially having your product commingled or having your product delayed because you did not follow the rules on labeling your product. A product can have multiple UPC codes; make sure to cover them all.

Mistake #19: Not using Discount Cards or Programs

When you source your product online or at a store, you should use discount cards, coupon or rebates sites. Not doing so, means you might be leaving money on the table. There is a website called Raise.com where you buy discount gift cards.

If you are sourcing online, use websites such as Ebates.com where you can use a browser extension and get discounts for various online stores. Use a credit card that has rewards. In the end, you might be able to make money simply by using a combination of these and any other discount or reward system. Remember, you are competing against other sellers, and every little bit counts.

Mistake #20: Not keeping your personal and business bookkeeping or accounts separately.

If at all possible, try and keep separate accounts for your business expenses. For example, you might have a credit card that you only use for business. A separate checking account for business purposes.

Mixing personal and business expenses or deposits in the same accounts is not the end of the world, but keeping them separate will help you tremendously when you are doing your taxes. It also helps keep your bookkeeping focused so you can easily run reports on your personal accounts and business accounts separately.

Mistake #21: Not paying taxes on your income.

Again, we have mentioned before keeping track of your business expenses and revenues throughout the year. We talked about paying sales taxes. Now we are talking about paying federal income taxes at the end of the year.

Amazon will send you a 1099-K form when you have $20,000 in unadjusted gross sales. So your income is reported to the IRS. You will need to add this information when you fill out your taxes. If you make less than that, technically you are still required to pay taxes. You should discuss all of this with your CPA.

You might avoid paying taxes for years, but you might later be liable for past year taxes and might get penalized. Don't risk it. Keep track of your expenses and income and do what's right. In the end, you might not even owe any taxes, depending on how you did a particular year.

One more reason why you should keep track of all your expenses (See Mistake #xxx) because you can also claim your expenses. And if you have a lot of expenses that offset your income, you won't have to pay taxes. In the end paying taxes means one thing: you made money, and from that money, you can give Uncle Sam it's share.

Again, talk to a tax professional and decide what to do.

Mistake #22: Not doing proper packaging of fragile items

You have to prepare and send fragile items to Amazon in such a way that they will pass a drop test. When you send the products of Amazon, think of your customers. If the product gets damaged during shipping, Amazon may not notice this right away. You make a sale, only to have a quick return by your customer. Your defect rate goes up, and you may get bad seller feedback.

All because you did not spend the extra time to prepare your items properly. Learn the ways to package your product for Amazon FBA. Follow the rules; they are there for a reason.

Conclusion

Selling on Amazon FBA is very competitive. We must be agile and adapt quickly to changes. One thing that we should always do is stop and think about what it is we are doing. Check how are things going in the business.

When selling on Amazon FBA, periodically we should analyze what has worked and what not, so that we can determine how to move forward and continue making money. We want to be agile, but at the same time, we do not want to be making the same mistakes that others have made.

I hope that this book has proven useful to you. I hope that you will take the lessons in this book to heart. My sincere desire is that you will prosper in your business and that I can have a part in that by providing resources that will benefit you.

If this book has been of use to use, please let us know. Stop by our website and see what's available. Subscribe to our newsletter so that we can keep in contact.

Thanks for reading this book.

Do you have a minute?

If you enjoyed this book and want to leave us feedback, please take a moment to go to this book's product page on Amazon, scroll down and click on the "Write a customer review" button to leave us a review. We appreciate your thoughts on our books.

Paul D. Kings

About the Author, Paul D. Kings

Paul D. Kings is a Software Engineer, Father, husband, and self-published author. He likes to write about selling and making money online. Paul has been selling on eBay and Amazon since 2007.